Poems for
COMFORT
and
HEALING

Poems for
COMFORT
and
HEALING

SMITHMARK

For all those people who have recently or at some time in
the past lost someone they loved.

I bequeath to you, the living,
All joy and all sorrow.
Have courage always,
And sometimes, sometimes,
Remember me.

And in memory of my grandchild, Jordana Julia Mills,
aged six months, who died 31st July 1980.

INTRODUCTION

W hen a person or a family has to face the death of someone they love, they are unprepared for the depths of feelings that overwhelm them. They have never been prepared in any way for the situation in which they suddenly find themselves.

We live in a society in which death has become an unmentionable subject and in which displays of any kind of emotion are not socially acceptable. Women are allowed to have more feelings than men, but boys are trained very early to be 'manly', that is, not to cry, not to show they are hurt, and not to be tender and gentle. Some of my male clients have not cried since they were small boys and what a task it is to undo this suppression so that they can cry about the things that need to be cried about in their lives.

Some bereaved people, therefore, hide their feelings of loss and despair, put up a brave front for the world and for their families and struggle on. Some become ill or take to drinking, overeating or drugs to blot out the awful feelings inside. Suppression is, of course, the most psychologically dangerous way of handling the grief. Others find the experience of bereavement too intense to be able to suppress, so they have to find ways of living through it. All too often they feel totally isolated, immersed in their pain and do not know who to turn to for help.

In the past, many people were able to look to the comfort of their religion, to the psalms and other religious writings for some kind of solace. Today, however, many have little contact with organised religion or with any set of beliefs that might help in a time of such crisis. More than this, they do not even have any of the rituals that religions provided to allow the natural grief to be expressed.

Another problem that the bereaved quickly become aware of is that some people are unable to confront them. They are avoided or jollied along with drinks and cups of tea or told to pull themselves together. The loss that has completely shattered their lives and is the total focus of their attention, must not be mentioned.

Doctors, psychiatrists, families and others are firmly of the opinion that the loss of a loved one should be got over in a few months or a year. If the bereaved person is still grieving after that, then they consider there is something seriously wrong with them. Very often the bereaved are given drugs to lessen the pain. These, of course, only deaden the grief for a time and do not get rid of it.

As a psychotherapist, I know that the only way to handle grief is to express it and that if grief is not worked through it will be carried around by the person like a burden for years, taking its toll in depression and illness. I have had many clients who are still weeping inside for the baby they lost years before, for a husband or a wife or a lover who died and was never fully mourned. I think it's very possible that we never totally get over the death of someone we love but, if all the feelings can be expressed whenever they come to the surface, then we can begin to live again. We need to be able to have the grief, the fear, the guilt, the anger and the questions such as 'Why did they have to die? Why did this happen to me? If only I had done this or that.' All these things need to come out and be talked about. Hopefully you can find a grief counsellor you can talk to or an understanding friend who can just listen and not tell you what you ought to do, or you can let it all flow out into a private diary as did C.S. Lewis when his wife died. Or you can pick up a book of poems such as these and weep your way through them, knowing at least that someone else has felt as you are feeling.

I have made this book of poems because I think there is a need for it. This need was brought home to me very personally with the sudden death of my six-month-old grandchild and from my growing contact with parents who have lost their babies through the Sudden Infant Death Syndrome. I also lived through the sudden loss of my husband when my children were small. I would have found a book such as this valuable and comforting. I hope it will prove useful to others in their times of loss and despair.

There are many ways of living through bereavement, but if the loss can be fully experienced it can give, to those who go through it, compassion and understanding and add great depth and meaning to their lives.

Marjorie Pizer, 1992

NOTE

In the eleven years since *To You the Living* was first published, a greater awareness and understanding of the needs of the bereaved has developed. Bereavement counselling has become a normal part of the helping professions. There are now counselling services for police, ambulance officers, doctors, nurses and the general public who become involved in mass accidents, terrorist acts and natural disasters such as earthquakes. There is, therefore, a much wider demand today for a book such as this to be republished.

When this book was sent out for review in 1981, one Australian medical journal refused to review it because both the reviewer and the editor considered it too dangerous to be put in the hands of bereaved people. I was shocked by their attitude. Since then, *To You the Living* has been used widely in the helping professions. It has brought comfort to countless bereaved people and poems from it have been reprinted in anthologies, books and works on bereavement in Australia, USA, England and Ireland.

Seven new poems have been added.

Marjorie Pizer, 1992

CONTENTS

સ્ટ્

Bereavement and Loss

Despair and Healing

Bereavement and Loss

Your Death

The terrible devastation of the tearing apart
When you died so suddenly, so quickly—
There were no goodbyes, I was not even
    with you.
You were gone by the time I came,
Soul flown from its earthly shell.
Yesterday a warm, living man, loving, caring,
Today a body, cold and abandoned—all
    life gone.
How could I believe you dead, you who were
    so alive,
My dearest companion for seventeen years?
Gone, gone, gone and I left to carry on.
How could I live with such a wound?
My soul torn apart, how could it ever heal?
What devastation and grief entered my life
On the day you so unexpectedly ended yours.

A Father Dead

I cannot speak to my children about
    their father—
He is lost to them and to me.
Therc is an cmpty space where a father
    should be.
There is an empty space where a husband
    should be.
There is a sea of grief between me and
    my children
And I cannot speak of their father.
Perhaps they think that I have forgotten him
After all these years.
It is just that I cannot speak of him
Because of all these tears.

After Seven Years

Seven years you have been dead
And it is like a lifetime.
Sometimes I wonder
If you ever really happened.
Sometimes it is only yesterday
And I know that I will never again see your face
Asleep on the pillow beside me,
Never again see your head bent close over
    a book,
Never again hear your voice quietly talking—
And then I know
That I will always carry the scar
Of your sudden and too-early dying.

The Existence of Love

I had thought that your death
Was a waste and a destruction,
A pain of grief hardly to be endured.
I am only beginning to learn
That your life was a gift and a growing
And a loving left with me.
The desperation of death
Destroyed the existence of love,
But the fact of death
Cannot destroy what has been given.
I am learning to look at your life again
Instead of your death and your departing.

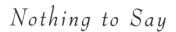

Nothing to Say

When he spoke of your death tonight,
Silently I cried to myself, 'no, no, not again!'
My eyes were full of tears—
I could not speak
When he spoke of that day.
I could only listen and cry inside
And go away.
Tonight, even after nine years,
When he spoke of your dying
I could only cry.
There was nothing at all that I could say.

Dream

Last night
I dreamt my olden lover back from the grave
And in my arms again,
As if the years of death were but a dream.
He was as young as he was then,
But I was grey and older, as I am today.
I lay within his arms, comforted
   and comforting,
Forgetting in my dream that he was dead.
I had almost forgotten his gentle face
And the touch of his hands and his voice.

The Train Park Revisited

Here in this park I sit
And fifteen years have passed
Since last I visited it,
Since I sat here
To watch the trains go by,
And count the carriages,
Under a cloudless sky.
The children laughed and swung on swings,
The hours flew by on rushing wings.
Now I am returned again
With tears in plenty shed,
Both children having grown and fled—
Their father ten years gone and dead—
And here I sit alone and watch the trains go by
And cry.

Anniversary

Today, if you had lived,
You would have been fifty-six,
But it is only I who have reached it.
Sometimes, after all these years,
I feel as if you never really existed.
Sometimes it seems only yesterday
That we were young and full of years to come.
For seventeen years you were the companion
    of my body and my soul.
I have had lovers since, and friends,
But always I will remember you
With gladness and with sadness
On this, the anniversary of your birth.

Funeral

Wattle and almond blossoms picked
   from home
For the tiny coffin of my grandchild.

Reminders

There are reminders of the dead
    child everywhere—
The cot, tossed and empty, that had become
    a deathbed—
Folded nappies awaiting tiny limbs now cold,
Shawls and clothes, carrying basket and pram.
There is the mother crying terrible tears,
Her breasts hard and aching,
Full of milk never to nurture the little one lost—
Her arms empty of the small, warm body,
Her heart irreparably torn.
There is the young father comforting
    the mother,
His own eyes red with grief,
His body taut with shock,
Holding the few photos and talking of his child,
The fact of death unreal as yet.
There are reminders of the dead child
    everywhere in this house.

Dying of Cancer

I cannot stand the agony of your dying.
I cannot even imagine what it must be like
To be trapped in a body racked with pain and
   desperate illness,
With no knowing how long the final escape
   will take.
It is not the death but the process of dying,
The agony that must be lived through with no
   one willing to shorten it,
And the watchers wringing their hands with
   helplessness.

Empty House

I must get used to coming home to an
    empty house,
To find no welcoming presence waiting for me,
No cosy lights and kettles boiling
For companionable cups of tea.
I loved coming home, knowing that you
    were there,
Working or writing and awaiting my return,
Both of us equally pleased to see one another.
Now I must become accustomed to coming
    home to an empty house.

It is so Hard to Remember

It is so hard to remember that you are dead.
At any moment you could walk into the house
Just as if you had been up the street shopping,
Or had just finished some writing.
Despite the fact that I walked with you
Every inch of the terrible path of your dying,
Sometimes, still, I cannot remember that
    you are dead.

End and Beginning

O you, who have returned to the infinite
    beginning
From whence we all have come,
Having made an end of what was begun many
    years ago,
Have you become a star in some
    undiscovered galaxy
Or are you a breath or a breeze
In the in-breathing and out-breathing of
    the universe?

Out of the Crashing Thunder

Out of the crashing thunder of the storm,
The cyclone at the centre battering my soul,
Cliffs of fall and I have fallen, frightful, sheer.
Comforter, where, where is your comforting?
O who am I, being wrought out of fire
    and tears,
Out of the wild sky and the dying,
Out of the tempest of my love?
Who am I, that am being tempered with fierce
    anguish and loss,
And making poems to comfort my poor heart?

For my Mother, Long After her Death

Forgive me, mother, for I have sinned.
I blamed you, in my blindness, for many things.
I held you off all my life, pushing you away,
Never allowing you near.
Only now I know how dear I must have been,
Though you could never say.
Only now do I see.
You gave me time and space and books,
Music, a room of my own and poetry.
You found me hard to understand
And I was intolerant with the sharp intolerance
    of youth,
Rejecting all that you valued.
Forgive me, mother, wherever you are,
For taking so many years to see
All that you did for me.

Memories of my Father

Throwing my mind back to my childhood,
I think of those now dead
Who people my past.
I think of my father,
Dead these forty years and more,
A silent, solid man
Who fled the Czar of all the Russias
To preserve his life and later, mine;
Who, quite unknowing, saved his whole family
    from war,
From the ghetto and the gas chamber.
All I remember is a quiet man,
Remote from children, not easily questioned,
Who died before I could ask him
All that I wanted to know.

Evanescence

(WRITTEN AFTER THE DEATH OF MY
YOUNGEST BROTHER)

Tonight I feel the evanescence of life—
Now it is here and then it is gone—
Passed into the air like a piece of music,
Played and then heard no more.
All the solidity of everyday happenings,
The strength and beauty of people,
The weight of houses and buildings
And all the physical things that surround me,
Have become airy and insubstantial,
Made only of jostling particles of nothingness.
I feel as evanescent as a cloud, a leaf,
An insect or a wind—
Here and solid today, I, too, will be swept away
On one of the coming tomorrows.

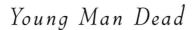

Young Man Dead

It is a beautiful night, warm and still.
The city buildings are glowing like palaces
And people in cars,
Gay on their Friday night pleasure,
Drive about alive and well.
But the young man is cold in his coffin
And his family sit and grieve.
What can I say to them who are bereft
   so suddenly?
Who can give meaning to so cruel a loss?
The young man lies cold in his coffin
Whilst we who are left, weep and live on.

Anniversary Lament
for Joan

This time last year
The boy was here—
Painting the shed,
Going to bed.
This year no more
Will he pass the door,
Will he read a book,
Will he sit and look.
He is dead,
With all unsaid,
With little done—
Your son.

Garden of Remembrance

(THIS GARDEN HAS A ROSE BUSH FOR EVERY
MAN FROM THE DISTRICT KILLED IN THE
PAST THREE WARS)

Walk quickly past the roses,
Walk quickly past the names,
Walk quickly through the tears.
Do not remember the sons who are lost,
Do not think on the friends who will
    never return,
Do not remember the husbands who will never
    come back,
Do not recall the dreams undreamt,
The lives unlived,
The love unloved.
My eyes are full of tears—
I cannot read the names.

O gardener,
Why do you dig another bed
To plant more roses in?

(THIS POEM WAS WRITTEN DURING
THE VIETNAM WAR)

Collaroy Beach

Here I am, this sunny morning,
Sitting by the green winter ocean,
Watching the sun catch the breaking surf
    with gold,
Watching the darting gulls,
The black-rubbered board-riders
Gracefully riding the waves,
The families picnicking on the grass
And wondering, wondering—
I have swum in the icy ocean pool
And sit warm and dressed in my car
In the midst of all this movement of water
    and people,
Pondering, pondering—
How is it that I sit here,
So strong and full of life,
When the husband of my friend,
Younger than I am,
Sits at home in a wheelchair slowly dying,
Having become an old man in a few months?
Sitting here, facing the continuity
Of the ocean, the beach and the sky,
I ponder on the living and the dying
That each one of us is here to do.

For my Cousin, Nancy

When finally I said goodbye
She cried hard sobs like a little child
And tears came to my eyes
For she is old and ill and vague,
But somewhere deep she felt we might not
    meet again.
She held my hands in hers, smoothing and
    patting them,
But could not speak
And I was choked with tears
Remembering the years between us and
    the love.
My heart was heavy as I went away
And left her in her room.

Importances

O how important are all the things of life,
Friends and possessions, political struggles
And the future of the human race,
Scx and sport and who said what
    about whom,
And the job and the shopping,
And being tired and being happy
And being young and being old.
How important all the everyday things are
Until death steps near
And strips away all the paraphernalia which
    surrounds us—
Then all these importances turn into trivia
In the face of the great mystery
Of where we come from
And where we go to at the end.

For my Old Dog, Tippy

When I stood there
And held your head in my hands,
I saw life fading from your old brown eyes.
Your head grew heavy as you slipped away,
Your eyes emptied and were still.
As I held you gently, stroking your soft fur,
I was sobbing inside.
My eyes were full of tears.
Silently I said goodbye,
Going away from the strangers who
    were there.
Leaving you with them,
I took my grief to have alone
Where I could not be seen.

For Frisky

I miss you, cat, since you have died.
I miss your pattering feet
Running down the hall when I come home.
I miss your loud demand for food.
I miss your warmth sitting on my lap
And your loud purr of happiness.
I miss our talks and you sitting on top of
　　my books.
After seventeen years, old cat, my house
　　seems empty;
I miss your company now that you are dead.

My Dead

Today I have been thinking of all the dead in
    my life.
All my memories are stirred;
My private ghosts are rising
And my head is full of tears.
I had thought that they were all quietly
    bedded down
Deep in their old, forgotten graves.
But no, my ghosts are risen in their
    full strength
And are walking round with me,
Pulling me back into far years and past events.
Lie down, my ghosts, and sleep.
Every day I have enough cause to weep
Without your clamour from the past.
Lie down and sleep at last.

Tears of all the World

Why am I so choked with grief, so full of tears?
I have had sadness enough these last few years;
It is surely done and past.
But inside I have an ocean of grief
Welling up from some deep depths
Below my memory,
Weighing me down with the accumulated tears
    of centuries.
I find it hard enough to cope with my own grief,
But without help
I could drown in the tears of the whole world.

Lament

I am lamenting the loss of love in my life,
The friendships failed,
The friendships ended,
The family hardly known,
Father and brothers and mother,
Unreached, untouched.
I am lamenting the death of my beloved,
The ending that was not intended,
A man becoming a memory in a moment.
How my heart grieves for the dead ones
And the lost ones,
And how my heart leans out
To gather in those who are close to me.

Poem for a Parting

I am looking at you
So that I will remember your face
When you are gone.

I am listening to you
So that I will remember your voice
When you are gone.

I am being aware of you
So that I will remember how you feel
When you are gone.

I am busy saving you all up in my mind
Because I am afraid I might forget your face
If you are gone too long.

Despair and
Healing

Lost in Despair

Lately I have been letting my life
Fall into pieces about me.
All the old familiar ways have become
   meaningless.
I have been lost in despair's dark depths.
I have been lost in a forest of ills.
Wandering alone and calling for help,
I have looked to death as an escape
From the intolerable agony within.
Now it is time for me to turn from death
And chart another path.
Girding myself with courage and with hope,
I must find new tasks
And make a new beginning from an old
   and finished ending.

Into the Depths

Last week
I could have cast my life aside
Like an old shoe —
I could have ended my stay.
I cannot tell
How seas of hopelessness
Drowned my soul.
I could not speak
Of my wish for death.
I drew into myself
Like a snail into its shell
Wishing for an end.
I withdrew from those I love,
Not caring for them any more.
There was a devastation
In my inmost soul
And a terrible aloneness,
And I was smitten down
Into the depths of the abyss.

Retreat

Why does my spirit now and then
Fling itself down into the deep
Of despair?
Then I can only weep
For my own misery and wish
Myself alone.
Then I retreat into my own shell
And shut the world away
And have nothing to say.
And yet out there, all is well,
Sun shines, children play,
And I alone am out of tune.
Come, come, my heart, be brave,
Fight through this anguish soon
And reach for life again.

The Everlasting Sea

As I sit by the mighty ocean
Before the tumult of the waves,
I beat my breast
And cry at my hurt,
And still the waves roar in.
So will it be when I am gone,
When all my hurt and grief
Has been forgotten
In the sea of time.
When I am lain to rest
The eternal surf
Will wash this sand
Just as it does this day.
O everlasting sea,
Wash out my grief and hurt
And make me whole again.

Destruction and Creation

I have been to the edge of the abyss
And I have looked into the depths.
There I looked at death
And have returned to the living.
There I looked at madness
And have returned to the sane.
There I looked at destruction
And have returned to create.
For only creation and love
Can answer destruction and madness
    and death.

Overwhelmed

When I feel overwhelmed by destruction,
Let me go down to the sea.
Let me sit by the immeasurable ocean
And watch the surf
Beating in and running out all day and
    all night.
Let me sit by the sea
And have the bitter sea winds
Slap my cheeks with their cold, damp hands
Until I am sensible again.
Let me look at the sky at night
And let the stars tell me
Of limitless horizons and unknown universes
Until I am grown calm and strong once more.

Healing

I sat in my desolation
Withdrawn from all around,
Feeling my life was a ruin, a failure.
I was empty inside
With the utter collapse of my being.
I did not care any more
For living or dying.
I was alone
In my distress and desolation.
But as I sat sadly on the ground,
The sun reached out his hand to me
And touched my face
And so my healing began.

Strength

Inside,
I am making myself strong.
I am weaving bands of steel
To bind my soul.
I am knitting stitches of suffering
Into my hands
To make them strong.
I am strengthening my mind
With the warp and weft
Of weariness and endurance.
I am binding my faith
With the bonds of psalms and songs
Of all who have suffered.
In time,
I will be tempered like fine steel
To bend, but not to break.

Courage

Call on courage when fear engulfs;
It is provided in limitless loads,
Enough and more than enough for all.
Never forget to call up courage in times
    of crisis,
In times of terrible loss—
It is the lifeline out of the abyss.
When all else fails,
Call courage to your aid.

Stormy Waters

What stormy waters have I been sailing through
These past few months!
I have not known whether I would come to port
Or founder on the way.
What storms of heart and soul have I endured,
Tossed here and there,
So often in despair,
I have abandoned hope for all so racked and
    tempest-torn.
And yet, battered and tired,
Uncertain, shaken but still whole,
I limp to port for shelter and repair.

Rebirth

I am emerging from an ocean of grief,
From the sorrow of many deaths,
From the inevitability of tragedy,
From the losing of love,
From the terrible triumph of destruction.
I am seeing the living that is to be lived,
The laughter that is to be laughed,
The joy that is to be enjoyed,
The loving that is to be accomplished.
I am learning at last
The tremendous triumph of life.

Paradox

Do not be trapped in doom or despair,
Do not be overwhelmed by misery and ugliness
For behind all lies the immensity of
    the universe,
The incontrovertible beauty and perfection
Of every act and counter act,
The inevitability of an end begun in
    the beginning,
The inevitability of a beginning begun out of
    an ending.
Out of the multitudes of the many
Is born the ultimate unity.
Out of the underlying unity
Are born the million, billion, trillion manys.
None are one and yet all are one.
Do not be trapped by despair
For out of despair many a new flowering may
    be born.

Gifts

I must be what people call a sentimental person.
I have worn by dead husband's watch these last
    sixteen years;
I use my mother's old sewing scissors,
Dull, grey, sharp scissors such as cannot be
    bought these days;
I wear my grandfather's old sovereign case
On a fine chain around my neck;
I remember playing with it as a tiny child
As I sat on his knee.
And from my father I have mulga bookends,
The only present from him I ever remember;
From my great aunt, a long, thin spoon
Which I measure out tea with;
From my grandmother, I have a strange, old,
    very useful tool,
Hammer, screw-driver and pliers combined;
And from one great grandmother whom I do
    not remember,
An engraved silver spoon,
Early symbol of my fortune in this life.

I love the continuity of all these things,
Knitting my past into my present,
Linking the living with the dead.

They have each left me a gift and a
    remembrance,
The completion of a circle which makes
    me whole
And strong to continue on.
I, too, will leave gifts and remembrances
For the continuation of those who will come
    after me.

Web of the World

In the whole web woven of the being of
    the world
Each of us has a place,
A small corner of the tapestry uniquely ours,
Spun in with our times and those around us.
We weave our own corner into its own shape
And all the tiny shapes become the whole,
And the whole moulds the little shapes
Until all are become part of one another.
No matter how small, all are required;
No matter how unimportant, all are necessary;
Each touches the whole and becomes a part
    of it.
Even you, even a small lizard, touches
    and changes
The skirts of the universe.

Remembrance

When I die
Will you be sad that I have gone,
Sad that our friendship has ended,
That our talking is over,
That we have parted? —
Remember me.

When I die
Will you be glad that I lived,
Glad that we met,
Glad that we enjoyed so much? —
Remember me.

When I die
I leave you love and the sea,
Friendship and all the loveliness of the world.
I bequeath to you, the living,
All joy and all sorrow.
Have courage always,
And sometimes, sometimes,
Remember me.

I First Awoke

I first awoke
To the multitudinous cries of kookaburras
All along the wide river
Greeting first dawn.
I awoke again with the sun striking my eyes
From over the mountains,
Calling me to be up and out
To the lush bush,
To the tall white gums,
To the prawn boats
And the old graveyard.

The dew lay thick and wet
On the long grass among the graves,
And my dog bounded over them
Chasing butterflies and bees.
The old gravestones are tilting and sinking
Under the earth of the hill —
Old bones mouldering in old earth,
Making new earth and new life.
I could lie on such a quiet hill
By such a still, deep river
When my time comes,
And have dogs chase butterflies and bees
Over my discarded bones.

First published in the United States in 1992
by SMITHMART Publishers Inc.
16 East 32nd Street
New York, NY 10016

by arrangement with Collins/Angus & Robertson Publishers Pty
Limited, Sydney, Australia

First published in Australia in 1992,
under the title *To you the Living*, by
Collins/Angus & Robertson Publishers Pty Limited
(ACN 009 913 517).
A division of HarperCollinsPublishers (Australia) Pty Limited
25 Ryde Road, Pymble NSW 2073, Australia

ISBN 0 8317 6798 7

Printed in Hong Kong

5 4 3 2 1
96 95 94 93 92